Acknowledgment
The editor and publishers would like to thank Mary Haselden for her help in selecting rhymes for this book.

British Library Cataloguing in Publication Data
Chamberlain, Margaret
    Numbers.
    I. Title
    398'.8
    ISBN 0-7214-1115-0

First edition

Published by Ladybird Books Ltd Loughborough Leicestershire UK
Ladybird Books Inc Auburn Maine 04210 USA

Printed in England

numbers

illustrated by MARGARET CHAMBERLAIN

Ladybird Books

1

One little cockerel
Bright and gay,
Stood on a gate
At break of day.
"Ho, little cockerel,
How do you do?"
"Quite well, thank you.
Cock-a-doodle-doo."

One little green frog in a pond am I;
Hoppity, hoppity, hop.
I sit on a little leaf high and dry
And watch all the fishes
As they swim by –
Splash! How I make the water fly!
Hoppity, hoppity, hop.

Two little blackbirds
            singing in the sun,
One flew away
        and then there was one;
One little blackbird,
            very black and small,
He flew away
        and then there was the wall.

One little brick wall
            lonely in the rain,
Waiting for the blackbirds
        to come and sing again.

A little brown rabbit
        popped out of the ground,
Wriggled his whiskers
        and looked around.

Another wee rabbit
        who lived in the grass
Popped his head out
        and watched him pass.

Then both the wee rabbits
              went hoppity hop,
Hoppity, hoppity, hoppity, hop,
Till they came to a wall
              and had to stop.

Then both the wee rabbits
              turned themselves round,
And scuttled off home
              to their holes in the ground.

Two fat gentlemen
Met in a lane,
Bowed most politely,
Bowed once again.
How do you do?
How do you do?
How do you do again?

Two thin ladies
Met in a lane
...etc.

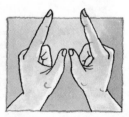

Two tall policemen
Met in a lane

...etc.

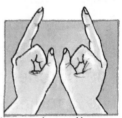

Two little schoolboys
Met in a lane

...etc.

Two little babies
Met in a lane

...etc.

Rub-a-dub-dub,
Three men in a tub,
And how do you think
They got there?
The butcher, the baker,
The candlestick-maker;
They all jumped out
Of a rotten potato,
'Twas enough to make a man stare.

Three little ghosties,
Sat on three posties,
Eating buttered toasties,
Greasing their fisties
Up to their wristies.
Weren't they beasties
To make such feasties!

Four currant buns
            in a baker's shop,
Round and fat
            with sugar on the top.
Along came a boy
            with a penny one day,
Bought a currant bun
            and took it away.

Three currant buns
            in a baker's shop

...etc.

Two currant buns
            in a baker's shop

...etc.

One currant bun
            in a baker's shop

...etc.

Five little soldiers
Standing in a row,
Three stood straight,
And two stood – so.
Along came the captain,
And what do you think?
They ALL stood straight,
As quick as a wink.

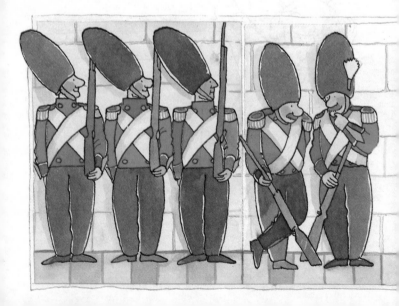

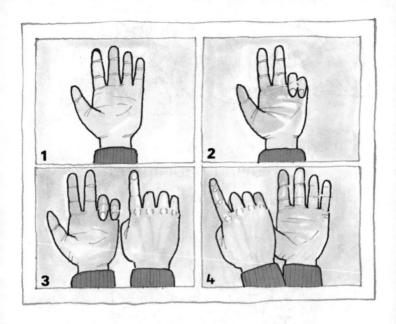

Five little pussy cats
       playing near the door;
One ran and hid inside
       and then there were four.

Four little pussy cats
       underneath a tree;
One heard a dog bark
       and then there were three.

Three little pussy cats
      thinking what to do;
One saw a little bird
      and then there were two.

Two little pussy cats
      sitting in the sun;
One ran to catch his tail
      and then there was one.

One little pussy cat
      looking for some fun;
He saw a butterfly
      and then there was none.

Sing a song of sixpence,
A pocket full of rye;
Four and twenty blackbirds,
Baked in a pie.

When the pie was opened,
The birds began to sing;
Now wasn't that a dainty dish,
To set before the king?

The king was in his counting-house,
Counting out his money;
The queen was in the parlour,
Eating bread and honey.

The maid was in the garden,
Hanging out the clothes;
When down came a blackbird
And pecked off her nose.

One potato, two potato,
Three potato, four,
Five potato, six potato,
Seven potato more.

One, two, three, four,
Mary at the cottage door;
Five, six, seven, eight,
Eating cherries off a plate.

Eight brown teddies
                sitting on a wall.
Eight brown teddies
                sitting on a wall.
And if one brown teddy
        should accidentally fall,
There'd be seven brown teddies
                sitting on a wall.

Seven brown teddies
                    ...etc.
Six brown teddies
            ...etc.

Five brown teddies
                    ...etc.
Four brown teddies
                    ...etc.
Three brown teddies
                    ...etc.
Two brown teddies
                    ...etc.
One brown teddy
            sitting on a wall.
And if one brown teddy
            should accidentally fall,
There'd be no brown teddies
            sitting there at all!

9

Higgledy Piggledy,
My black hen,
She lays eggs for gentlemen;
Sometimes nine,
And sometimes ten,
Higgledy Piggledy,
My black hen!

There was one little, two little,
   three little Indians,
Four little, five little,
   six little Indians,
Seven little, eight little,
   nine little Indians,
Ten little Indian boys.

One man went to mow,
Went to mow a meadow.
One man and his dog, Spot,
            and a bottle of pop,
Went to mow a meadow.

Two men went to mow,
Went to mow a meadow.
Two men, one man and his dog, Spot,
            and a bottle of pop,
Went to mow a meadow.

Three men went to mow,
Went to mow a meadow
                    ...etc.

Who built the Ark?
Noah! Noah!
Who built the Ark?
Brother Noah built the Ark.

Now in came the animals
    two by two,
The hippopotamus
    and the kangaroo...*etc.*

Now in came the animals
    four by four,
Two through the window
    and two through the door
        ...*etc.*

Now in came the animals
    six by six,
The elephants laughed
    at the monkey's tricks
        ...*etc.*

Now in came the animals
　　eight by eight,
Some were on time
　　and some were late

...etc.

Now in came the animals
　　ten by ten,
Five black roosters
　　and five black hens

...etc.

Now Noah said,
　　"Go and **shut that door!**
The rain's started falling
　　and we can't take more."

This old man, he played one,
He played nick-nack on my drum,
With a nick-nack paddy-whack,
Give a dog a bone,
This old man came rolling home.

This old man, he played two,
He played nick-nack on my shoe

...etc.

This old man, he played three,
He played nick-nack on my knee

...etc.

This old man, he played four,
He played nick-nack on my floor

...etc.

This old man, he played five,
He played nick-nack on my hive

...etc.

This old man, he played six,
He played nick-nack on my sticks

...etc.

This old man, he played seven,
He played nick-nack up to heaven

...etc.

This old man, he played eight,
He played nick-nack at my gate

...etc.

This old man, he played nine,
He played nick-nack on my spine

...etc.

This old man, he played ten,
He played nick-nack once again

...etc.

One, two,
Buckle my shoe;

Three, four,
Knock at the door;

Five, six,
Pick up sticks;

Seven, eight,
Lay them straight;

Nine, ten,
A big fat hen;

Eleven, twelve,
Dig and delve;

Thirteen, fourteen,
Maids a-courting;

Fifteen, sixteen,
Maids in the kitchen;

Seventeen, eighteen,
Maids in waiting;

Nineteen, twenty,
My plate's empty.

Oh, the grand old Duke of York,
He had ten thousand men.
He marched them up
            to the top of the hill,
And he marched them down again.

And when they were up
            they were up,
And when they were down
            they were down,
And when they were only
            half-way up,
They were neither up nor down.